BRIGHT IDEAS TO MAKE YOUR

WRITING SPARKLE

By: Sheila S. Hudson

www.sheilahudson.website
sheilahudson.writer@gmail.com

Sheila J
Hudson

Chapter 1

You Don't Send Me Flowers Anymore

When viewers see writers portrayed on the movie or television screen, they are depicted as having a pretty "glam" job. They are wined and dined by the powers that be, the female writers get rooms of roses, and their names in lights. Studio executives whisper their names with reverence. Okay maybe not the last one, but you get the picture. Screenwriters are often authors who have jumped from the jacket cover of their best seller to tinsel town. They get the photo shoots with celebrities, cocktails at The Club, dinner at Sardis, and conduct interviews with television and radio hosts. You get the picture.

But the truth is, by and large we writers are a quiet, introverted shy bunch. If we are very fortunate, while we scribble our hearts out, our spouse or significant other sits in the shadows, pays the bills, and bolsters our more-often-than not sagging ego. A writer under deadline is dangerously waffling between writer's block or working feverishly to capture an idea before it evaporates. Writers thus engaged are dangerous to approach. It takes courage, patience, and old-fashioned "hard-headedness" to coexist with a person so unbalanced and downright weird.

Living with a freelance writer is serious business. A person who voluntarily fills that position must realize that any conversation, scandal, gossip tidbit or secret is fair game. A snippet may end up in a short story, feature, essay, or newspaper article. An important aspect as the writer's significant other is to filter what the writer in residence is privy to. Your sanity may depend on it.

A desperate writer can squeeze 1,000 words out of taking out the garbage. A writer in a deadline crunch can modify personal experiences with gusto, even embellishing and expounding on the insignificant until the desired word length is achieved. Family vacations, reunions, and social gatherings are not exempt. Vacation for a writer is not down time. In fact, for a humor writer it is a prime opportunity for gathering column ideas. Writers are never "off." They continue to write regardless of the locale or climate. The new unfamiliar surroundings may even spur the writer to exciting new genres. Day to day routines may lose their luster for many, yet a truly creative writer with too much time on his hands can lift the mundane to ludicrous and beyond. Living with a writer isn't easy but it is always interesting.

Even the most conscientious may occasionally allow wedges of half-truth and smidgeons of innuendo to creep into a supposedly unbiased article; it therefore lies at the feet of the writer's keeper to rein him in when things get out of hand. A writer on a word binge is no different from an alcoholic; he has no grasp on reality and cannot rest until said manuscript is put to bed. This same wordsmith is compelled to begin another manuscript immediately else the blank page will mock both his dreams and leisure time, thus adding stress to your otherwise carefree life. I know of what I speak.

My husband, Tim, and I have been married for 50 years. We are both writers in different venues. Several years ago, the two of us agreed on some basic household rules.

Never approach a writer who is sitting in silence and ask, "What are you doing?" Said writer will take offense because they are working out the layout of their next article while all the while you may suppose that they are daydreaming.

And as an addendum, when you observe the writer watching a favorite television sitcom, N**ever assume they are relaxing but rather working out plot formats and transitions, looking for plot points and complications**.

With many years of free-lancing cohabitation under his collective belt, my spouse husband willingly wallpapers my office with rejection slips, resubmits returned manuscripts, and stubbornly refuses to allow me to wallow in writer self-pity. Instead he points to the calligraphy sign over my study door: *If you would not be forgotten, either write things worth reading or do things worth the writing.* (Ben Franklin)

Soon he and Ben have me tapping away at the keyboard. With support like this, I can readily overlook the fact that Tim doesn't send me flowers as much as he used to. However, he buys laptops every other year, thumb drives by the dozen, color cartridges by the truckload to feed my printer that scans, copies, faxes, as well as prints.

Tim and I travel to interesting places where I interview people for a column. We both get special treatment with our press passes. Tim takes photos when I require them for travel columns; he hauls books, prints maps, and is always positive and generous with his encouragement and support.

Once while I was speaking at a retreat, he surprised me with a roll top desk that he had spent an entire day putting together. That was when I knew I had arrived as a writer at least in his eyes. That desk is now crammed full of completed writer's courses, manuscripts both accepted and rejected, rejection letters, and articles which have been printed and reprinted. My writing materials overflow to the bookcases, filing cabinet, and closet. I have a desk top and a laptop computer, access to cable Internet service, and a library of resources plus a generous allowance to writer's conferences.

While I might not get as many floral arrangements, I now possess my own offices. I am no longer resigned to a corner of our bedroom with a pad and ballpoint. Now that I think about it, a lot of my writing dreams have come true and a lot of that is due to my husband's faith in me. Maybe I should send Tim flowers.

Chapter 2

Think like a Writer

In the hilarious comedy, *My Blue Heaven*, Steve Martin portrays an informant being protected from the mob by the FBI. When one of his "get rich quick" schemes fails, he is left with thousands of five-gallon water containers instead of the intended "hot" merchandise to fence. Martin's character, Vinnie, takes one look at the back of the van and exclaimed, "Now the difference between us is that you guys see a mistake, but what I see is an opportunity!"

That's what I'm talking about. Not fencing stolen goods, but looking at situations skewed, cockeyed, upside down, sideways or askance. Any angle just so it's different. Sharon McDonnell gave us an excellent example of this in her nonfiction workshop at the Southeastern Writers Workshop. She noticed a pattern of amenities in airports like maps, interesting sculptures, and spa services while traveling both in and out the country. With a little research, Sharon parleyed her findings into a clever query and scored a top assignment. That's the kind of inquisitiveness a free lancer must have to compete and even thrive.

Thinking like a writer means taking notes, being observant, eavesdropping, and always being in the writer mode. Even on vacation, writers are always writing (at least in their heads). Could this be a story? Does this fit into my novel? What magazine would be interested in this subject? And when we come up dry with the resources available to us, we network with other writers to get their opinions, experiences, and critiques.

Often when I think I am on top of my game, my husband will point out something that he feels would make a good article. That very subject in plain view has usually escaped me. Ideas are always circling us. Like children with butterfly nets, it is our job to chase the fluttery ideas, hoping to catch a few and develop them into stories with strong leads, robust middles, and fabulous endings. Like Vinnie, we must be cautious not to think of what life brings as problems, but great opportunities.

If an "opportunity" seems just too much, consider collaboration with another writer. "Strength in numbers" may be an old saw, but never is it truer than in writing. My co-writer, Amy, and I have turned problems into opportunities with an hour-long meeting and a large cup of coffee. Editors are always looking for fresh perspectives and a friend looking at the same scenario may be the one to give it.

For most of us, ideas are not the problem. Taking the time to develop an idea, pitch the concept in a one-page irresistible query letter, and do the necessary follow up is often where we fail. For most of us, writing is not our primary profession and time is limited. That's when we need to use every resource available – working smarter not harder.

One way we can do this is use the same set of facts, figures, quotes, (research) for more than one article. Recently I had an assignment to do a piece on autism from a personal point of view. My grandson, Michael, was diagnosed with autism at 19 months of age. In my research I gathered more than I could use in the original assignment, so Amy suggested a compatible article for a woman's magazine, and I queried another source for an inspirational article based on the same subject. Working on this premise while collecting research, ideas for articles can take on many dimensions and the doors that open could surprise you (but that is an article for another time).

I am trying very hard to take my own advice. One year after some hurricane-produced rains, we experienced some leaks – plural. First, a toilet then a shower. A trickle came through the walls, ruined the kitchen and dining room floor, the ceiling, and finally a closet. We had the shower ripped out, the toilet repaired, and the kitchen floor replaced. But in the meantime, we found some copper pipes that needed to be replaced and a floor that had a few rotten places.

At the same time, the cable and Internet service went out. We replaced the modem and the router with still no service. When I complained to my writing partner, she smiled and said, "If there is humor in there, you will find it." I am still looking for the humor, but time plus perspective will help me find it. My daughters used to say, "Mommy, is this one of those things that will be funny one day, but right now isn't?"

But in *My Blue Heaven*, Vinnie takes his semi full of five-gallon water jugs, pastes a fake charity name on them, and places them all over town. He proceeds to set up an operation to collect the jugs, roll the coins, and deposit the donations. With a little ingenuity, Vinnie turns what could be a disaster into profits -- money in the bank. And so, will you, once you become proficient at translating problems into opportunities as you think like a writer.

Chapter 3

Writing Opens Doors

Several years ago, I met Kathy Trochek, a successful mystery writer, at a writer's conference. Kathy paid her writing dues at the Atlanta Journal Constitution as a reporter. Asking questions came second nature to her. I don't remember a lot about that class, but one thing I will never forget is her recounting of being granted admission to a fur vault in Rich's, a prestigious department store then located in downtown Atlanta.

Kathy explained to the Rich's authorities that in order to make her fiction believable, she needed to view an actual fur depository in order to write a believable description. Voila! Not only did she gain entrance, but the officials allowed her to take measurements, photograph the areas not vital to security, and interview a few the personnel. Kathy's entertaining sideline to the class taught me a valuable writing lesson: **Being a writer opens doors**. All kinds.

One year when my husband and I registered for a World Science Fiction Convention in Boston, I casually asked for press credentials. My reasoning was this: I DO write a monthly column for Athens Banner Herald. True, it is a travel column but usually the topic is within driving distance of Athens. I knew if they pressed the issue, I might have a problem. Without a blink, the convention registrar bestowed credentials that ushered me into a much-celebrated exhibition on the Lord of the Rings trilogy and landed an interview session with a renowned writer plus gave me certain prestige among the badge wearers. After all, I had an interesting brown ribbon on my name badge instead of the usual colors. My sidekick and faithful companion, Tim, went along as photographer and got the royal treatment as well.

While I would never advocate misrepresenting yourself in order to gain entrance, I find that many times we reclusive spend-too-much-time alone types are overly modest about our accomplishments and talents. It is merely a matter of putting your best foot forward. After all, if we were writing credentials for someone else, wouldn't we make them shine?

Another writer friend got to ride along in a police cruiser as part of her research on a police procedural mystery. Those of us in her class asked how she accomplished that, she said, "I just asked."

For instance, if you are on assignment for a newspaper or a magazine, it is appropriate to say so and state what information you hope to gain. Only once was my word challenged which was quickly resolved when I promptly produced an editor's name with her telephone number.

Affiliations with easily recognizable publications like *Guideposts* or *Chicken* S*oup* may help you gain admission, get the interview, or whatever research data you are requesting. Just be sure that what you say is true and that you handle the situation in a professional manner. Obtaining entry under false pretenses will surely come back to haunt you.

In my tenure as a writer, I have found that people are fascinated to meet a "real" writer. Most people don't give a thought to who composes the obituaries, pens the crossword, puts together the research for the magazine article on AIDS, or who prepares the text for the 11o'clock news. The general population spends 24 hours a day 7 days a week surrounded by a world of words created by us – writers.

Writers of fiction or nonfiction, well known or obscure, published or in progress, are fascinating creatures to the average populous. Some of them live under the delusion that we are quirky, highly intelligent, and well traveled individuals who are enchanting conversationalists. I, for one, do my best to foster that fantasy. It can come in handy when you run into a snag, need specialized research, or a special favor.

And, who knows perhaps you may choose to name a character after that kind librarian or drop a meaningful gesture into your story as a tiny homage for services rendered? A thank you on the dedication page or a mention in the footnotes will guarantee passage for research on the most obscure subject.

One entry into the information world you might not consider is the Internet. As for me and my house, we can't do without it. I research a lot of my travel articles on the web, especially those I don't have the time to explore in person.

Most web pages have a tab labeled media or press info or a button marked "contact." Go on that page and request a media kit for that source. Media kits are free and contain a gold mine of facts, year-end reports, brochures, and many times include pictures for media use. This information is updated frequently and available by snail mail or to download and print on your own.

Prose opens portals. Epistles of truth provide egress into amazing worlds. Even graffiti opens word gates and gives a peek into cultures different from our own. Yes, friends, writing opens doors but the first one it opens is your own.

Chapter 4

Never Throw Anything Away!

Okay this is not an original idea. One year at the Harriett Austin Writers Workshop in Athens, Georgia, I sat in on a session taught by Terry Kay. This master of literary fiction told a story of creating a character named Lottie. She was a beloved character with a charm that he knew would be an integral part of a story. The problem however was that she didn't "fit" what he was writing at the time.

No matter. Coming from a drama background, Terry realized that he had something here and carefully crafted the character of Lottie giving her attributes to make her a believable, endearing personality. Lottie embodied a combination of traits

Terry valued in people both real and imagined. When Lottie was finished, she possessed virtues and quirks. She had loves and those she despised. Lottie had endured many losses and only a few triumphs. She was appealing in many ways. When Terry was satisfied with his character, he filed her away for several years.

He explained that he began the story with another name as the central character. Then when he remembered the Lottie character, fully fleshed out, he realized she was perfect for this story and he changed the title to reflect it. "See," he reminded the class, "Never throw anything away. As a writer, you will come upon a time when you need it." When the time was right, Terry Kay wrote his best seller, Taking Lottie Home.

It is true. The more years that I write and the more varied my prose, I find that I can reread an article, a journal entry, a dialogue, or an exercise, and insert my present self into that time frame for a re-experience of an emotion. Even a clustering exercise can get my brain churning on a subject in order to recall an experience I thought I'd long since forgotten. Clustering by the way is an excellent way to come up with an essay, column, or break writer's block. Another trick I use is reading the dictionary.

Another excellent way to "keep" everything is in a writing journal. Last week, I was bored or procrastinating (not sure which) when I decided to reread some of my journals. I was ashamed at some of the awful first drafts, amazed at a few of the short pieces and one pretty good poem, and astounded that I found a great 1,000-word article on pet resurrection.

No. I am not going Stephen King on you. This story is one every parent can identify with -- how a child's pet dies and the parent secretly replaces it so that the child doesn't know. My daughter and her husband did this scores of times with our grandsons' two goldfish – Zip and Dorothy. Anyway, the point being that this perfectly good unpublished manuscript was sandwiched between a poem about peanut butter and jelly and a commentary on vacationing in Canada. Because I had recently noticed that Chicken Soup was advertising for entries to be collected in a volume entitled Chicken Soup for the Mothers of Preschooler's Souls, I polished my pet story and in less than an hour and released it off into cyberspace.

That is just my experience. I'll bet most of you have a few stories, poems, screenplays, or manuscripts tucked in your closet, collecting dust bunnies under your bed, or stuffed into a desk drawer that need resuscitation, perhaps a little editing, and some TLC.

Keep in mind that markets and editors change. What gets rejected one time under one regime may do very well when the power shifts. Just be sure that the editor who rejected it the first time doesn't receive the same manuscript a second time. That is a big NO-NO.

Another reason for never throwing stuff away is that if you diligently file (a foreign word in some circles) your creations in folders, after a few years you will have a collection of articles on a single subject. Thus, you can compile, edit, and publish your own anthology, collected works of poetry, or short story collection with a similar theme. For example, I have been compiling, collecting, reading, and writing on the theme of forgiveness for years. I prepared a book proposal on this subject and am now ready to proceed. This is an interest of mine that has been on the back burner while I wrote magazine articles, profiles, travelogues, essays, interviews, and the like. When the theme of forgiveness emerged in my writing, I grouped it in my "special collection."

Not everything you write will get published nor should it be, but it is fodder for the works of art that will follow. Remember, don't throw anything away not even a poem about a peanut butter and jelly sandwich.

Chapter 5

Use Life Experiences as Fodder

"Where **do** you get your ideas?" I am sure you'd like to have a dollar for every time you've been asked that question. No matter what genre you write, the story begins with a kernel of an idea. Every interview of an author that I've read contains that question in some disguised form. Non-writing muggles have a theory that eventually writers run out of ideas. I know I did.

When I first began writing in 1992, I imagined that one day I would go to my computer and alas there would be nothing to write about. But if I have learned anything in those intervening years, it's that the MORE you write, the MORE you must write about. As soon as I foresee the "no idea" prophecy about to come true, I turn another corner or rather fate throws me into a "situation."

One example is when I got an earplug stuck as we landed in Honolulu. I spent the first few hours of my 30th anniversary trip at the airport clinic. I get screams of laughter at this story, but people invariably ask, "Did that really happen?" I get the same reaction for my menopause stories, the accounts of our haunted light fixtures, and tales of our neighbor's dog, Einstein, who crashed through our picture window.

My "situations" began at a young age when my cousin, Linda, and I emancipated Horatio, the prize bull. We spent the better part of the evening chasing him in a cornfield on a moonlit night.

Another time my Uncle Roy dressed up like Santa and got stuck on the roof. Yes, they are true. I couldn't make up anything that bizarre if I tried.

But wait! There's more. I was bitten by a baby black bear while on vacation, lost in the Washington, D.C. Capitol building, and kissed by the award-winning actor, Henry Winkler, at the Music Box Theater in New York. Life just keeps handing me these treasures. When life hands them to me, I write about them.

Not all life hands me is positive. In 1982, Tim and I had our moving van stolen en route to Georgia. That was a trial I eventually wrote about, but it took me ten years to get the courage. And just like anyone else, our family has weathered its share of illness, divorce, betrayals, and challenges.

Before I became a writer, I didn't know what to do with all these episodes. After a few retellings, there was nothing to do but retire them. Ah! But now I record them for posterity.

If I am fortunate, some of them find their way to a periodical or anthology while other more mundane occurrences remain in my journal. Perhaps one day they will be fodder for a grandson to write a novel, a screenplay, or just have a good laugh at Mimi's expense.

Either way writing provides an extra "eye" with which to view the event – a tip I picked up when I was first learning to write. Writing is therapy to work through the bad stuff or celebrate the crazy bizarre situations you may discover along life's highway. Either way a writer's life is the best life of all.

Recently I spoke to a creative nonfiction college class. We covered the newspaper column, essays, personal narrative, profiles, and other standards of the craft. In closing, the inevitable question was asked, "Where do you get your ideas?" I simply told them the truth, "They just come to me."

Chapter 6

Don't Give Up The Dream

Never. **Never. Never. Give up.** Successful writers never give up their dream. If you do, you can't get it back. Harlan Ellison says there are a few secrets in the field of writing.

*"First is the big secret. The one no one ever tells you. And it is this: anyone can **become** a writer. . . The trick is **staying** a writer."*

Faulkner was a postal employee. King bussed tables at a seafood restaurant and was later a school custodian. Tom Clancy sold insurance. John Grisham practiced law. But one thing they all have in common, they continued to write.

Ernest Hemingway encouraged: *"Work every day. No matter what has happened the day or night before, get up and bite on the nail."* Most of us have written enough to know that the only way to get better is to write more.

Ross Perot, statesman and once presidential candidate, said, "Most people give up just when they're about to achieve success. They quit on the one-yard line. They give up at the last minute of the game one foot from a winning touchdown."

Mr. Perot's observation encourages me. Once I've fulfilled the writing and editing phase, then comes the biggest test of perseverance – getting rejected by publishers. Jack London was rejected 600 times before his first story was published. Louis L. L'Amour was rejected 200 times. Irving Stone received 16 rejections for "Lust for Life" and it later sold 25 million copies. Pearl S. Buck, George Orwell, and Norman Mailer received their share of rejections too. So did Grisham who ended up self-publishing and we know the rest of that story.

Many of us have occupations other than writing by which we earn a living. Still we turn our "hobby" into an avocation – something we are passionate about. Madeline L'Engle had over 30 rejections for A Wrinkle in Time which is now considered a children's classic and won a Newberry Medal in 1963. Ms. L'Engle expresses that *"Writing is like eating or sleeping. I'm not fully human unless I'm writing."* Like the rest of us she squeezed in time around family, career, and other personal responsibilities. She persevered and so must we.

Bottom Line. Write the best possible prose, poetry, or play that you can. Edit, revise, rewrite, and polish. Get rid of the "ly" adverbs, use action verbs, cut adjectives to the bone, and obliterate unneeded verbiage. Put your darling manuscript in the neatest, most precise format ever and send it off to its destiny. Then quickly get to work on something else.

Remember Churchill, the English bulldog, and "Never give in! Never, never, never. Never – in anything great or small, large or petty – never give in except to convictions of honor and good sense." Enough said.

Chapter 7

Swing your Partner

Writers write. It's what we do. Some writers carry around a pen and pad of paper. Some keep writing implements in the car and beside the bedside table. A writer I know has a pen with a light so she can write when the muse prompts even if it's in the middle of the night. This is a good habit to acquire early to capture gems overheard when around children.

"A three-year old child is a being who gets almost as much fun out of a fifty-six-dollar set of swings as it does out of finding a small green worm." (Bill Vaughn) As the grandmother of seven I know the truth of that statement. Children ask questions; they inquire. Kids savor the moment of here and now and do not worry about the future or what might take place next.

Children are great writing partners because they have wonderful imaginations. Andrew and Cooper once had a collection of dogs and stuffed animals. Both middle children, they each had a unique ability to come up with colorful and sometimes weird names for their pets – like Chocolate and Brownie. But just when you think you see a pattern, one of them comes up with Bead-o. Children also have great memories especially the pre-readers.

Hudson, our grandson and resident math genius, memorized the bus numbers of all his friends. My best friend's grandson learned all the presidents of the United States and in order. How many kids do you know who pretend to be Rutherford B. Hayes and Millard Fillmore?

"It is not a bad thing that children should occasionally and politely put parents (and grandparents) in their place." (Collette) Critiques keep us humble, help us employ simpler dialogue, and force us to explain terms in a more elemental vocabulary. For a writer, this is not a bad thing. Children are painfully honest, guileless, and maybe the most innocent opinion you can get.

One of my mentors said he often told a story to a child and asked them to repeat it. Then he would adapt his version of the article to the easier vocabulary. If the child didn't understand the content, chances are neither would the people reading the material.

"You can learn many things from children. How much patience you have, for instance." (Franklin P. Jones). Rachel Carson said, *If a child is to keep alive his inborn sense of wonder, he needs the*

companionship of at least one adult who can share it, rediscovering with him the job, excitement and mystery of the world we live in." Youngsters have a natural sense of wonder. It is our duty as writers to foster that. If you are lucky like me, you have access to children that you can partner with. If not, borrow one. Because somewhere in our growing up, we tend to lose delight in living, wonder, and awe. We must recapture it and nurture it in others. As a bona fide card carrying, grandmother of the Magnificent Seven, I have a sworn and solemn duty to uphold silliness in any form, nurture expression, and encourage love of language.

Gore Vidal once suggested, *"Never have children, only grandchildren."* He got it right!

Chapter 8

The "F" Factor

During recovery from surgery, I took pen in hand thereby launching myself into a world of wonder, fear, and hope. To help other struggling scribes, I am penning ground rules discovered in my writing quest. I choose to label them, "Sheila's F Factors."

The first "F" stands for **Freelance** writing. Freelancing conjures up a wonderful fantasy of a mistress blowing kisses and beckoning from a distance doorway. She promises fame, fortune, and financial freedom. Like the star of an adventure film, we in the craft fearlessly pursue our mistress down dark corridors, through secret passageways, and along treacherous heights to claim the prize, solve the puzzle, and ride off into the sunset with her and a hefty check from a publishing house.

When fantasy wears off, we encounter "F" number 2: *Fear*. Fear can be a good thing if it doesn't block your creativity. Instead use fear to fuel your writing. In Stephen King's "On Writing" he advises, *"The scariest moment is just before you start. After that things can only get better."* Use your greatest fears, angst-ridden memories, and embarrassing moments to make your writing interesting, detailed, and engaging.

Family is "F" number 3. Cleverly disguise members of your family and incorporate their quirks into a character for one of your writing projects. I had an uncle who talked to himself, told himself jokes, and laughed outrageously at them. Those of us raised in the south tend to possess colorful relatives. Use them as comedy relief, sidekicks, or to create a poignant scene. This principal also applies to Foes.

Relish *Funny* situations, "F" number 4. Use everyday happenings to create short personal narratives, memoir chapters, or magazine fillers. I came home from work one afternoon to find the large, black poodle next door had plunged through my window in order to get to our cocker spaniel. Our house had attracted a crowd of onlookers since the burglar alarm was blaring. Our neighbor apologized profusely and arranged for replacement post haste. It was an unusual evening to say the least. Nevertheless, I used the illustration in a talk because the very unintelligent poodle was named Einstein.

As hard as it is to admit, we all fail at something. So, make *Failures*, "F" number 5. Use failed relationships, poor job choices, bad decisions, and any secrets you can disclose without a lawsuit. Make them a character's foibles or a personal confession story. Tears in the writer equal tears in the reader. If your writing can evoke emotion in the person who reads the material, you are a success no matter what the publisher pays you.

And don't forget this one – *Fantasy*, "F" number 6. Imagination is wonderful. Feed it with good literature like the Harry Potter series, The Chronicles of Narnia, the Lord of the Rings trilogy, science fiction, adventure stories, or cozy mysteries. Whatever your reading taste, give your character idiosyncrasies but don't make him too odd. Jessica Fletcher, the main character in "Murder She Wrote," is a widowed schoolteacher who doesn't drive. Nero Wolfe is an obese genius detective who solves crimes without leaving his home. Colombo, a police detective, drives a broken-down car and wears a trademark trench coat year-round. Ironsides conducts investigations from a wheelchair via his staff. Adrian Monk, my favorite TV detective, uses his obsessive-compulsive disorder to put away criminals in the San Francisco. Incorporate enough traits to make them lovable, but don't overdo them lest the traits become annoying.

And finally, "F" numbers 7 and 8: *Flair*

and Finesse. Write with depth of meaning, weave in plots, back story, description, and important facts. Don't hit your reader over the head with too much at once. Establish your own unique voice. Try writing the same story from first person and again from third person. See which works best. Don't be afraid of using "I".

Follow the sage advice given Stephen King from his college literature professor: "When you write a story, you're telling yourself the story. When you re-write your main job is taking out all the things that are NOT the story." Consequently, he continued, "Write with the door closed, and re-write with the door open." Once you know what the story is and get it right, then it belongs to anyone who wants to read it. And that's what writing is all about in the first place, getting our story from our imagination to the readers'.

Chapter 9

Write With Your Veggies

Dieticians tell us that nutrients contained in orange juice promote healthy the skin. Doctors advise that carrots improve one's eyesight. But did you realize that okra can help you to be a better writer. My friends from the low country will no doubt agree, but for the others, let me explain.

OKRA is a vegetable, that's true. And without okra it's just not gumbo. But OKRA, I have discovered from reading author, Nancy Callahan, is also a wonderful revision process. Nancy suggests in Absolute Write, an online publication, a method which is simple and involves reading through your draft four different times. Each time you read through your manuscript, your assignment is to focus on a different function. I have included her suggestions and made a few of my own.

O is for OVERVIEW, OMIT, AND OVERWRITE. The first draft will be wordy, give a broad picture, and contain stuff you will need to omit. That's why first drafts were invented. Just to get the story out. Comb through the manuscript for the first time searching for punctuation and syntax errors, redundancy, vague or unneeded adverbs, excess words or phrases, clichés or trite sayings, unnecessary or vague information, weak dialogue, or confusing flashbacks. Pay attention to transitions and use only passages that move the story along. Keep in mind your target audience and concentrate on their point of view. Above all, don't make the mistake of falling in love with your own words.

"The great American writer Thomas Wolfe was famous not only for his quality of his prose but also for its quantity. He had a brutally hard time cutting excess words from his drafts. 'Although I am able to criticize wordiness and overabundance in others,' Wolfe wrote to his editor Maxwell Perkins about his novel Look Homeward, Angel, 'I am not able practically to criticize it in myself. The business of selection and revision is simply hell for me – my efforts to cut out 50,000 words may sometimes result in my adding 75,000.'".

I suppose that is why his first draft of Look Homeward, Angel came in at over 1,000 pages. Wolfe and Perkins kept at it until they pared it done to 750 pages.[1]

The **K in OKRA stands for KEEP**. Keep what

---

[1] The Complete Idiot's Guide to Writing Well, Laurie Rozakis, p. 17.

is the story and leave out what is NOT the story. Retain precise phrasing and strong dialogue. Built the concrete details and keep only those sections which you feel you cannot improve upon. Be picky and strict on what you select to keep. If you have reservations about a section of the story, try rewriting it or leaving it out altogether.

About editing yourself, William Faulkner advises, "All the trash must be eliminated in the short story, whereas one can get away with some of it in a novel."[2]

R stands for REVISE, REWORK, and REWRITE. Look at deleted sections and decide if they belong, go over punctuation, grammar, subject/verb agreement, verb tense, dangling modifiers, bland nondescript adjectives, weak verbs, passive voice, excessive use of prepositional phrases, sentence fragments, and run on sentences. Look over your sentence structure and vary sentence lengths. Nothing is more boring than twelve sentences the same length and all beginning with "the." Give your prose variety and rhythm by mixing simple sentences and complex sentences. Do the same with paragraph structure. Avoid stereotypes in developing your character sketches, show don't tell throughout, don't settle for anything less than a compelling introduction. And be sure to include a satisfying conclusion, don't just stop! Each scene in the story should add to the tension and push the plot toward a climax. Don't confuse your reader with point of view, be consistent throughout the piece.

---

[2] On Being a Writer, edited by Bill Strickland, p. 146.

This section requires a lot of attention to detail. Don't be like Peter DeVries who is quoted as saying, "I love being a writer. What I can't stand is the paper work."

The **A in our acrostic stands for ASK, ACTION, and ADD**. The final time you read the manuscript ask yourself what it might be lacking. Is there enough action? How did you handle crucial scenes and important details? Are the characters memorable and likable? Do you give the reader basic character and setting details so that the story is appealing to all? Although the brainstorming stage is past, if you find a glaring hole add the missing ingredient to the pot.

Simmer your gumbo. After the initial **OKRA** exercise, put your manuscript away for a few days. Work on something else. After a reasonable length of time, repeat the **OKRA** drill. You may need to do it more than twice in order to meet your own criteria for a flawless manuscript. Just like the soup, writing flavor improves when left to simmer and meld the flavors of experience, memory, and insight.

Your mother never let you, but now that you are all grown up. Play with your veggies and boost your performance as a writer.

Chapter 10

Networking

I get by with a little help from my friends –
Lennon/McCartney

This quote brings back nostalgic verses from the popular Beatles era when many of us were in our formative years. For writers, it should be our daily mantra.

Productive writers can no longer, if they ever could, exist in a palatial ivory tower turning out prolific poetry and prose without contact with others. Even the most hermit-prone scribe must occasionally reach out via the telephone, email, or snail mail. When that happens, both parties are surprisingly enriched.

In my fledgling days of writing, I was timid to show what I had written to anyone. Then I experienced an amazing epiphany: writers are for the most part a compassionate, encouraging tribe who flourish through the propagation of our kind. Even doses of criticism are quickly followed by praise. A positive note from a writing instructor kept me writing for a year and continued to fuel my desires of being a "real" writer someday.

Later in my writing endeavors, I noticed that instructors, fellow scribes, and internet buddies are willing to take valuable time away from their own projects in order to assist with writer's block, help solve a plot problem, or suggest markets for a manuscript, or offer help with yet another rewrite. Money can't buy expertise of this quality. Via long distance and in person, I have received help with book proposals, verb tense, voice, and point of view – my own writing weaknesses. And not all the conversations are negative, sometimes my mentors tell me my dialogue is great, the title is funny, or the story is interesting. This gives me hope that indeed I will finish and submit this manuscript. It might even get published!

When I was a newcomer in the writing community, I mistakenly thought that only those who wrote my type of prose could appreciate my writing and consequently were the only writer friends who could help me. Not so, often those who write in a completely different genre can be your best editors and/or proofreaders since they read with a completely different slant. Each time I received a critique formally or informally, it was followed with the advice: *remember YOU are the author and YOU decide what stays, what gets cut, and what final manuscript version gets submitted.* However, other opinions are valuable even if you choose not to take all the advice offered.

On one occasion, I went through a rough patch after writing an essay on my family. A mentor that I respect gave me her advice and helped me get another perspective on this deeply personal issue. Friends of that caliber are priceless treasures. I hope everyone reading this column have someone like that. If not, make it a goal to adopt a writing buddy for just such times.

On another occasion, I had rewritten a magazine article until all my objectively was depleted. I began to despise the manuscript, and everything related to the project. Finally, in desperation, I reached out to a journalist friend. She cut through (literally) the frills and dug out the real story line. My returned article bled with red ink from her surgery, but I met my deadline with a piece I could be proud of.

Networking is one of the best tools in a writer's toolbox. Stephen King suggests in his book, *On Writing*, that each aspiring author build his own writing toolbox. The primary tools are vocabulary, grammar, and style. But just behind the basics is networking, an excellent tool for those times when you need information from an authority. Teaming up with an expert is a win-win situation. You get the research data you require for completing your article, the co-author get credentials, and the reader profits from both.

My spouse and I have written as a team on several occasions when requested to address opinions concerning campus trends, the future of campus ministry, and how to prepare your child for university life.

Another idea many of you may not have entertained is to team up with a child. I have gotten some great ideas and wonderful quotes from my seven grandsons. Especially those of you who write inspiration or juvenile, child like perspectives are pure gold. I've gotten answers to my questions about God, forgiveness, love, heaven, brownies, music, and stinging bugs. Children are a pure source of knowledge not to be overlooked. They can also ask questions and expound philosophies that keep you awake at night.

And don't forget the ultimate networking: reading. Stephen Kings gives his prime rule: ***"Write a lot read a lot."*** How else can you get excellent mentors undisturbed by time or distance? An open-minded writer can learn from anyone and anything if he keeps his antennae tuned and relies on *"a little help from friends."*

Chapter 11

Be a Word Nerd

*The difference between the right word and the almost right word is the difference between **lightning** and a **lightning bug**. Mark Twain*

If you are a writer, you must love language. You must love language not just enough to use it in the trade but take the time to understand it, even at times romance it. There are no short cuts when it comes to selecting just the right modifiers, prepositional phrases, and worse tense. As writers we vow our allegiance to continue the Order of the Mystery of Well-Chosen Words. Good humor writing for example uses prose that changes speeds, jumps up and down, and sneaks up to surprise you in order to deliver the joke. The very words that read so easily and glide off your tongue are the ones which required the most work and careful planning in order to pull off that ease.

I may be preaching to the choir when I say for the umpteenth time you've heard it: **Writers must be readers** - readers of others' works as well as your own. It is imperative that you can read what you've written with clarity. We possess an individual reader in our head independent from the writer who is also in our head. And if that isn't a big enough crowd, we also have an editor in there as well. These three entities are not going to always agree since they have different functions, temperaments, and levels of awareness. **Stay with me here.** When rewriting and editing your manuscripts, the (internal) editor and the (internal) writer must work together to deliver the perfect manuscript for you, the reader.

The best thing about writing is that we can always change the words. The worst thing about writing is that we can always change the words. Some writers board a carousel of rewriting that spins until doomsday unless there looms a deadline. So, if you don't have an official deadline, **give yourself one.**

When the writer and the editor think the reader is going to love something but once on paper the words get in the way, true professionals (like us) must enjoy fiddling with the words until they are perfect.

Here's Roy Blount, Jr.'s view on the craft: *If you are not a bit of a word nerd, like a computer nerd, I don't see how you can stand to write. It's like trying to stack up firewood. You have one piece that won't fit in. You love the piece, but it won't fit in the sentence one way or the other. You switch the sentence around, fool around with it back and forth, and you get sick and tired of it and go to the next sentence. Meanwhile, you are looking at the last sentence and then you go back and work on it some more, but then when it does pop, it's nice.*

Developing your own unique writing voice is a process. And you must love the writing process for the craft to be a joyous experience. Getting just the right word in the perfect spot make take all the resources, patience and skill you possess but there's nothing better.

I am sure many of you have pulled an article out of a pile of clips, began reading, and said "wow, this is good!" Then much to your chagrin, you look at the byline and blink because it's your name there. It's that euphoric moment that writers live for.

And back to the man who knew well the search for the right word, Mark Twain (aka Samuel Longhorn Clemens). *The right **word** may be effective, but no **word** was ever as effective as a rightly timed **pause**.*

Something to think about. (Pause)

Chapter 12

Don't Forget The C.A.S.H.

Bruce Barton's method for gaining inspiration was when his wife announced she was re-carpeting. He didn't enjoy the leisure of wrestling words. Necessity, the inner drive of creativity, and a low bank balance drives us ever go forward, makes us willing to risk rejection, compels us to agonize over every punctuation mark, and commands us to consume reams of paper.

Writers are a peculiar breed, but you already know that. We spend evenings writing personal experiences, memoir, or short humor columns while others frolic. If you are one of "us" I propose four points to check before handing your manuscript over to the editor.

1. **Don't forget** the **C** for **Circle**. The best pieces I have ever read (and can still remember) were written in a circle. The closing lines circle back to the opening lead. Notice that some of the most popular television shows use the same device. Something in us likes everything tied up

at the end. Whether the ending is happy or not, it must satisfy the reader. In my "Mama Always Said" stories I set up a situation with an anecdote and end with one of the tried and true "Mama Always Said" clichés only with an added zinger twist. Your regular readership will look for that, don't disappoint them!

2. **Don't forget** the **A** for **Aha!** Those who have written for Chicken Soup, Chocolate for Women, or other similar series know that the "goose bump ending" is something the editor demands. The writer can't just solve the dilemma, there must be the Aha! Moment, the Eureka, the Epiphany but so artfully disguised that it isn't obvious (unless of course you are writing for a younger audience). **The Aha!** is often so understated that it can be overlooked, that's why every writer needs a writing buddy to point it out.

3. **Don't forget** the **S** for **Story**. Duh! That's elementary isn't it? Perhaps. However, I have been known to go on a tangent, be determined to use an illustration or quote, or my brain went AWOL and caused me to stray from the original intent of the piece. That's when you, the all-powerful author, have a choice to either "kill the darlings," change the focus of the article, write more than one article on the subject, or chuck the project. In order to avoid this post traumatic stress, give a lot of thought to titles, individual quotes, and the lead sentence. Those are the items that hook your reader and sell your story. Everything that comes after the lead must be relevant to the subject, not mystically linked in the writer's mind alone.

That's the only way to stay on target and please your editor.

4. **Don't forget H** for **Heart**. Whatever your purpose in the article, don't forget to include emotion. This may be accomplished through dialogue, innuendo in a character's behavior, using subtle weather cues in the setting, or other writer techniques. In my own nonfiction accounts, my goal is to prompt the reader to tears, laughter, provoke action, or produce a nod of fond recollection. If someone tells me they "laughed out loud" or my prose "brought them to tears," I have achieved my goal.

Yes. **C.A.S.H**. is a beautiful thing, an anachronism that can bring you success and assist you in your life of wrestling with words. Mr. Olin Miller said, *"Writing is the hardest way of earning a living, with the possible exception of wrestling alligators."*

Make sure you get combat pay.

Chapter 13

Become a Hunter-Gatherer

Primitive societies survived under a system of hunters and gatherers who kept a fresh supply of needed commodities streaming into the communal storehouse. The arrangement necessitated the hunter and/or gatherer going into the wild, foraging and hunting in order to bring home the bacon.

In modern society, roles have changed. In the olden days when the hunter-gatherers exhausted the range of raw materials for food, tools, weapons, clothing, and shelter they moved on to another location and the cycle began again. I think there is a lesson here. Writers can glean a lot from the hunter-gatherer sequence. From this point on, consider yourself a hunter-gatherer. You are a hunter of fun, facts, and full out adventure.

If for instance, you take a vacation, avail yourself of brochures featuring out of the ordinary sites, jot down notes on restaurants and museums, and eavesdrop on interesting conversations. Make a note of that amusing anecdote your friend shared at a dinner party. Capture in a succinct word picture a toddler's attempt at playing the guitar or making a bouquet of the neighbor's hyacinths. With the electronic age, it's easy to put these musings in folders under specific categories rather than throw scraps of paper into a desk drawer never to see the light of day.

When you are deep into that essay and feel it needs a punch or something to make it authentic, pull out that quote or anecdote that just fits. When the prose needs lightening up, insert comic relief with something amusing you picked up in a family reunion. And nothing adds to your writing like description whether it is a few well- chosen words about the gargoyles on Notre Dame or a play-by-play of the basketball game at the local YMCA. There's just something about being there, taking it in, jotting it into your collective consciousness, and being able to reinsert it like a mental file into your document.

I can't tell you the number of times I have written an essay on something for no good reason. Perhaps I was feeling sentimental; maybe I needed to pour out a frustration, or just wanted to work out my own feelings on a subject – only to require that same essay in a future column. Think of it as a collection.

Collectors run the gamut. There are the usual ones like those who collect dolls, knives, plates, music boxes, stamps, trains, Civil War memorabilia, and so on. I recently just read about a man who collects mustard. That's right, mustard! He has 5,000 varieties and built a museum to display his collection.

So here is your assignment. Instead of a tangible collection of items, try collecting the following: sunsets, waterfalls, quotes from a child, ways to say hello, recipes for disaster, sunrises, memories, and things that give you goose bumps.

Take joy in what you collect, inventory them, but don't hoard them away. Share them with others, swap, and collect more. You don't need shelving, glass cabinets, or more storage for all you can gather. Let your writer buddies in on "scoops" you have garnered, writing workshops, classes, online markets, and opportunities for free lancing. It takes skill in both the hunter and the gatherer to make the system work.

And your second assignment is like unto it, get a writing buddy. Writing buddies critique, encourage, and bounce ideas (not manuscripts) off one another. If it weren't for my writing buddies, I would have given up in 1992. Try the hunter-gatherer method and you will be surprised how many times you will return to your "collection" for an embellishment to your original Bright Idea.

Chapter 14

All I Really Need to Know I Learned from My Writing Buddies

Robert Fulghum is one of my favorite authors. His nontraditional and sometimes off the wall humor makes me laugh and makes me think. In *"All I Really Need to Know I Learned in Kindergarten,"* he unveils "uncommon thoughts on common things." In rereading some of my favorite passages, I experienced a light bulb moment and saw how his twisted wisdom applied to the writing life. Here are his points coupled with some of my thoughts.

1. **Share everything.** Writers must network. When I attend conferences, I feel compelled to swap business cards, talk about

my manuscript "babies," and e-mail my deepest thoughts to fellow writers. I scribble notes on everything and share my opinions freely.

2. Play fair. Writers play fair. If I find a contest doesn't fit what I write, I have been known to forward it to a fellow writer whose prose fits like a glove. I like to think perhaps I have helped my friend get his big publishing break.

3. Don't hit people. Mama drilled into me that I don't physically hit others over the head but hurts still come in a subtler form. Writers exist on encouragement and ego bolstering. To have a writer friend we must be a writer friend.

4. Put things back where you found them. Enough said!

5. Clean up your own mess. Ditto.

6. Don't take things that aren't yours. Writers are in a constant love affair with words. So, I must constantly remind myself not to take words in a group (like a quotation) without giving a proper citation. Plagiarism is an ugly word. Professional writers always give credit where due.

7. Warm cookies and cold milk are good for you. And so is cold pizza – the breakfast of aspiring writers everywhere.

8. Live a balanced life. *"Learn some and think some and draw and paint and sing and dance and play and work every day some."* Thank you, Mr. Fulghum for that quote. When I forget to do these things, I steal a day away.

9. Take a nap in the afternoon. This is my favorite principal especially after a day of editing. Naps energize me as a writer and keep me from the grouchies during prime time.

10. When you go out into the world, watch out for the traffic, hold hands, and stick together. The publishing world is a big scary place for those of us aching to see our names on a byline. Without allies willing to steer me through the confusion of guidelines, agents, and the world of publishing, I would never have succeeded. I needed companions to hold my hand through seemingly endless rewrites, ruthless editing, a myriad of questions, and reward me with the 'atta girl' necessary for my existence. This mentoring, if you will, is only meaningful because it came from those of you who've been there before me.

Writers helping other writers. That's what I subscribe to. In 1993 I stumbled into a class and prayed no one would laugh at what I wrote. No one did and I've been writing ever since. I have gleaned a lot of knowledge and experience and every year it is my goal to give some of that to the new writers who come my way.

Mr. Fulghum distills his philosophy to "Be aware of wonder . . . remember the seed in the Styrofoam cup. . . All I really need to know about how to live and what to do and how to be I learned in Kindergarten. Wisdom was not at the top of the graduate school mountain, but there in the sand pile at Sunday School."

And to that, I can only add Amen.

Chapter 15

Google Yourself

One day I sat staring at the accusing blank page along with its condemning, blinking cursor, and I thought. Why not? I **Googled** myself. I called up the search engine and entered my name: Sheila Hudson.

Voila! In seconds, this little marvel spit out hundreds of wonderful diversions to meeting the next deadline. I found out there was a Sheila Hudson who is an athletic expert at the triple jump even competing at the Good Will Games and the Olympics. There is a Sheila Hudson in the United Kingdom and, yet another who is half-Korean.

But my most interesting name sake is the Sheila Hudson who is about my same age, has had a phenomenal weight loss, and is an artist living in Idaho. Did I mention that she is also raising her grandson?

The Internet makes this possible. Through its marvels I have become cyber pals (is that a word?) with the Sheila who lives in Idaho and have a standing invitation to visit.

Writers today live in a most blessed time as far as gathering information is concerned. At the touch of our fingertips, we can find population stats, define a word, research the history of a town, or locate a city in Siberia. We can see and talk to a relative in the Panama Canal via Skype, attach pictures to loved ones in Europe, or scan a document and send it across the sea or to the IRS.

No more snail mail to get lost, no more wondering if we have enough postage, and in many instances no more SASEs to enclose. My editors take my columns straight from E-mail with a Word attachment.

As you have heard from many wiser than I, there are stories all around you. All you must do is to be observant, listen, and occasionally **Google** yourself or somebody else to find out the details of that story.

Other interesting tidbits. I found a Sheila Hudson who is a journalist in Oregon, another who paints watercolors, another who is a personal chef, and another who is a personal trainer. Wow! A great legacy to live up to and what fun to find out what others with your name are doing in the world!

I am glad I didn't find any serial killers with our name. So, the Bright Idea solution to goofing off while snubbing your nose at the blank page is to **Google** yourself. You may just discover your tombstone in Milwaukee, Wisconsin and I've never even been there.

Chapter 16

Back to the Basics

A successful marriage requires falling in love many times, always with the same person. Mignon McLaughlin

My husband Tim and I have been married 50 years. To borrow a line from Jack Benny, "Not once have we had an argument serious enough to consider divorce; **murder**, yes, but not divorce." Fifty years has taught me many things, but one of the most important is it pays to go back to the basics. By that I mean, recall why you got together in the first place. I used to hang on every word that came out of Tim's mouth. I thought he was the most brilliant person on the face of the earth. I drove my family crazy spending hours in the bathroom getting ready for our dates. Hair and make-up, perfume, the outfit. Everything had to be perfect.

We used to take long walks and talk about everything -- our dreams, our failures, our fears. We enraged our parents by hanging on the phone for hours while as Tim and I watched an entire television program together. Our little in-jokes, our song, our restaurant, our first dance, the engagement, the announcement of the engagement. And on it goes. For the first year of our marriage, we celebrated every "month-aversary."

What happened? Life intervened. While our love isn't any less, our devotion and commitment levels are deeper and more resilient, our focus is different. Life tends to intrude with time crunches, family crises, health issues, financial concerns, not to mention the daily stress of living in modern society. It is then that we realize a need for a little R& R and getting back to basics.

It's the same for writers. Although we may have taken writing classes, audited courses, read books, published columns, articles, and maybe even written a book, our experiences may take us a direction we never intended. A return to the A, B, Cs of writing and a refresher course of the classics can never hurt. So why don't we return to the basics?

Sometimes pride gets in the way. We exalt ourselves above the fundamentals. But nothing could be further from the truth. Good writing is good writing whether it is in a children's picture book or a five-page spread in the New Yorker. The most excellent writers keep their craft fresh, their vocabulary crisp, and their stories filled with interesting twists derived from real life.

Another flaw in the writer persona is the ability to overlook and read into our creations things that we already know. The novice is unsure enough to read, re-read, ask others to read, and read again. When we have "arrived," we (meaning me) tend to skip that step, read the first draft, edit it, glance over it again, and send it out. Without careful line by line editing, that can lead to embarrassing mistakes. In a spa article I wrote for *Athens Banner Herald*, I mistakenly (don't trust spell check) talked about the facial I had and named the **anesthesiologist** instead of the **esthetician**. My editor asked if they administered ether or did I just fall asleep at the keyboard? Thank goodness she possessed a sense of humor.

A write getting back to the basics never refuses help from any source. Just because a writing buddy doesn't possess a box of clips doesn't mean they don't have good suggestions. Often, I have overlooked an obvious market or research source only to have it pointed out by a relative "newbie."

With apologies to the original source, *"A successful **writing career** requires falling in love many times, always with the same **muse.**"* Romancing your writing career like romancing a spouse means never tiring of whatever it takes to make the relationship work. Each time you reread the masterpiece in your hands or on your monitor, you'll discover other aspects of why you love what you do. And renew your vows to do whatever it takes to further your writing career and make your manuscript perfect.

Chapter 17

Set the Scene

Everything happens somewhere. Pieter Haag

In her *Guide to Fiction Writing*, Phyllis Whitney reveals that one of her little-known writer's tips is that she keeps a weather calendar. She takes an old engagement calendar with blank pages and makes regular entries. Some entries are just factual records of what blooms when and others are general observations.

One of her April entry reads, *Fuzzy soft green of a leafing willow tree. The winter landscape softly smudged as if an artist had rubbed his thumb across it. Trees not yet leafing, but no longer hard and bare.*

With a few brief sentences, Ms. Whitney places the reader in a setting and sets a mood. The emotion of her words has made you feel and see in your mind's eye a landscape as well as a longing for spring. You could also use a weather calendar to record a blizzard, a thunderstorm, or a very hot day. All of these would enable a writer to produce the mood for a specific time of year. Without noticing it, you place emotion when your original notation was made.

Another suggestion from Ms. Whitney is to visualize the setting you are aiming for. To do this you must sit quietly and watch it take place in your mind. Then as soon as you can after the visualization, record your sights, sounds, smells, feelings, emotions and anything else that may prove useful. Once done your weather calendar is there for handy referral when writing your prose.

Settings are always part of writing whether fiction or nonfiction. Think of the times that setting is a main character. *A Perfect Storm* and *Rebecca* are two that spring to mind. And where would Stephen King be without his famous *Christine*? No horror flick is complete without a house that has secret compartments, doors that creak, cabinets that open and close at will, or a ship guided by an unseen hand.

Even the clichéd phrase - "it was a dark and stormy night" – elicits a mood and gives you information. Film noir buffs know that a murder is taking place in black and white amid clouds of smoke in a dark back room. And once recorded, the setting becomes a part of that entire memory.

How could *Gone with the Wind* be set any other place but Tara and the Deep South? Would the *Blind Side* have the same impact set in France? My point is that settings include more than just description of place and time. They carry emotion, mood, horror, and maybe even the climax of the story.

Chapter 18

Making Magic with Your Muse

According to Stephen King, *there is a muse but he's not going to come fluttering down into your writing room and scatter creative fairy dust all over your typewriter or computer station. He lives in the ground. He's a basement guy. You have to descend to his level and once you get down there you have to furnish an apartment for him to live in. You have to do all the grunt labor, . . . while the muse sits and smokes cigars and admires his bowling trophies and pretends to ignore you.*

Do you think this is fair? I think it's fair. He may not be much to look at, that muse guy and he may not be much of a conversationalist (what I get out of mine is mostly surly grunts, unless he's on duty) but he's got the inspiration. It's right that you should do all the work and burn all the midnight oil, because the guy with the cigar and the little wings *has got a bag of magic. There's stuff in there that can change your life. Believe me I know.* (*Stephen King, *On Writing,* 2000)

And magic, my friends, is what we as writers are after. Getting in touch with our writing muse may seem strange to some but I've found that the creative spark sometimes needs a little special attention perhaps coaxing to get started.

If you want to entice the muse and get your work flowing, try one of the following techniques:

1. **Perform your own ritual before writing**. Light a candle. Take a bubble bath. Burn incense, pray, or meditate. This opens a spiritual door and unleashes the mysteries of your imagination. You may even type of write out a scripture, poem, or other piece that is meaningful to you.

2. **Carry paper and pen with you at all times.** Who knows? Your muse may give you an unexpected thought or you may become privy to an interesting conversation.

3. **Keep your journal handy.** I find that next to my bed gives me access for jotting down thoughts, prayers, interesting dreams, or ideas for titles. You never know when a story will come to you as a gift via your dreams.

4. **Take care of you**. Your body is the host for everything. Nothing takes the place of a healthy body, mind and spirit.

5. Surround yourself with positive, creative, and interesting people who support you and your writing career.

6. **Resist the urge for perfectionism.** This is one I must learn and relearn. Write first and edit later. The muse likes to visit when the inner critic is turned off.

7. **Enjoy life.** There's nothing like some down time to springboard ideas for future scripts.

I get a lot of ideas when I travel. It is the perfect antidote for boredom or the status quo. When I break away from my routine surroundings, I see things in a remarkable new way. Unique people and interesting places spark my creativity and make me grab for paper and pen. Whether you feel like writing or not, Stephen gives writers the following advice: *Your job is to make sure the muse knows where you are going to be every day from nine 'til noon or seven 'til three. If he does know, I assure you that sooner or later he'll start showing up, chomping his cigar and making his magic.*

Let's make magic with our muse.

Chapter 19

Bake a Better Cake

When I first started writing, I made a rookie mistake. I asked friends, colleagues, family, and minimal acquaintances to read everything that came out of my printer. In my naïveté, I was convinced it would only take me a few months to write the great American something or other.

What I didn't take into account was that in asking my inner circle to read advance copy usually one of two things happened: (1) either they read it and hated it but were afraid to tell me the truth, or (2) they read it and didn't understand it or skimmed it and protested that they loved every word. "Don't change a thing, honey. It's wonderful." (Relatives are more apt to do the latter.)

Either way it was an injustice to my readers. Friends' opinions are not going to be on the same level as an editors' unless of course they happen to be an editor. Family will either be blasé or occasionally outright mean. People not familiar with doing critiques will say things like "the beginning is interesting" or "the ending is perfect" which tells you absolutely nothing at all. Handing off a manuscript before it is ready is typical for a writing rookie, just be sure that you **never, never, never** give anyone a first draft to read. That's asking for trouble especially if you your thick writer's skin hasn't completely developed. And is it ever when it comes to family?

It didn't take me long to learn that prudence is the better part of valor or something like that. I gradually became more selective about handing out manuscripts to readers. Like every other writer each story, article, or personal narrative is "my darling" and must be protected against harm. Another pitfall is that if one adheres to the darling theory too ardently, you will soon begin not having critiques at all. A significant dip in income will attest that your editors aren't reading the "darlings" either, but speedily returning them in the SASE or reply e-mail.

I was reminded of this scenario from the e-zine, *Women on Writing.* I couldn't resist passing their wisdom on to my writing buddies: *If I bake a cake, and give eight people slices, and all eight people say, 'You should've used something called **'sugar'** in the cake mix.' Then I would be an idiot to yell out, 'No, this is how I made it. This is what came out. This was how it was supposed to be, and don't mess with my creative process!'*

Ouch that hit a little too close to home. How

often have we closed our notebooks (and our minds) to those who only wanted to help us become better writers? I decided to share their advice. "*I should take their advice and bake a better cake next time.*"

Time to stop reading the cook book and turn on the oven.

Chapter 20

Watch Out for Family

If you ever start feeling like you have the goofiest, craziest, most dysfunctional family in the world, all you have to do is go to a state fair. Because after five minutes at the fair, you'll be going, 'you know, we're alright. We are dang near royalty. Jeff Foxworthy

Family is the great equalizer. While all of us – even the toughest skinned writer – want our family to approve and even applaud our writing skill that probably is just not going to happen. Early on I learned that whenever I was published in anything, (a) my mother would declare it wonderful (before she even read it), my father would ignore it, my children would smile and pat me docilely on the head, but my husband (who had actually read it) would kiss me and reiterate how proud he was. Conversely when I had a manuscript rejected, my mother would declare that it was the publisher's loss, my children would smile and pat me on the head, but my husband would kiss me and say, "Congratulations you're a REAL writer."

Just about this time when I had been published and everything, the unthinkable happened. I began to write about my family, our relationships, our troubles, our vacations, our dysfunctionality (is that a word?). All was fine until horror of horrors; my family began to READ what I wrote. Who knew?

Then everyone got into the act. My mother told me to write about 'nice' things. My siblings asked not to be included in anything I wrote. My children requested that I change their names if I wrote about them. And I noticed that if I wrote anything – even a grocery list – in their presence, family members got edgy and noticeably quiet.

After two huge faux pas in my writing career, I offer this advice. **USE EXTREME CAUTION WHEN WRITING true stuff about your family**. You can write how to articles, humor if you alter names and highly exaggerate, inspiration if the outcome makes someone a hero, but if the plot involves flaws, struggles, skeletons in the closet, failures, and the like, you must be careful about putting it out there for God and everybody to read.

Pat Conroy wrote about his family. I understand that his father didn't speak to him for years and he and his siblings were estranged. I know the feeling. But I suppose becoming rich and famous with your fiction has a way of getting forgiveness from the hardest heart.

Stories that are close to the heart are hard to write as they conjure up all the old hurts, words spoken, and situations that make the writer uncomfortable. However, it is just those same emotions captured on the page that make the story valuable to the reader who may be living through a similar situation.

Not everyone has a dictator for a dad, a child with a disability, or a grandparent who survived a concentration camp. As writers we tell and retell the stories of our childhood in whatever way we can whether in art, music, poetry, or prose. We interview our relatives for information, emotion, and historical accuracy but some stories must wait to be told. Some adventures, romances, and mysteries must mellow with time enabling the storyteller to become sympathetic. Stories of this type must come full circle in order to help another individual with its telling. My family has its share of stories. Some of these have been told – funny vacations, poignant holidays, accounts of love and sacrifice, tales of heroism, and in them I am the star, the fool, the narrator, or the one who learns the lesson. I write them like I see them. Whether my relatives are portrayed as rednecks or royalty I will continue to describe them honestly, lovingly, and respectfully. I will also use them anecdotally and anonymously. But as for true stories about my next of kin, check my safety deposit box after my funeral.

Chapter 21

Change Your View Point

In the *Dead Poets Society (1989)* John Keating, played by Robin Williams, leaps upon his desk in front of the class and issues a challenge:

John Keating: Why do I stand up here? Anybody?

Dalton: To feel taller!

John Keating: No! [Dings a bell with his foot]

John Keating: Thank you for playing Mr. Dalton. I stand upon my desk to remind myself that we must constantly look at things in a different way.

. . . *Look at things in a different way* – that's what we as writers do. While others may view the same things we do, our writerly instincts give us a unique perspective.

In Alfred Hitchcock's *Rear Window* (1954), L. B. Jeffries, a wheelchair bound photographer, spies on his neighbors from an apartment window. It is from his unique perspective of being bound to a wheelchair and through the eye of his camera that a story unfolds.

As I write this column, I feel a like a combination of Keating and Jeffries. I fractured my foot on a cruise to the Bahamas a few years ago. One minute I was going to dinner with Tim, the next I caught my heel and my point of view radically changed. I dare say that nothing can change your viewpoint quicker than being wheeled off a cruise ship in a wheelchair or having a cane as your most noticeable fashion accessory.

The simple truth: there are places you can't maneuver, things you can't manage, and stairs you can't climb. Normal activities now bring agony and simple chores are left undone. A wheelchair surrenders you to another's care. It may be pleasant, or you may find yourself carrying packages and resembling a pack animal.

Compare that to using a cane. Walking with a cane is an art form. You must put the cane out first, then the bad foot which in my case was my right one, then bring your left foot past the injured one. Sounds easy, doesn't it? It wasn't.

It takes a bit of practice and a certain rhythm to progress. Shipboard I received a few nods, strangers opened doors for me to hobble through, other kind souls held the elevator. When Tim and I were together we received a few tsk tsks - which being interpreted is "Look at that pitiful couple both of them using canes." Quite a picture for our anniversary dinner, Tim sporting his bulldog cane with me clinging to the borrowed cane from the ship's medical center. A change in viewpoint had begun.

A cane is a very useful item. Not only can you walk with it, but you can use it to hook and drag items that are out of reach. A cane can get someone's attention with a gentle tap. It is useful to poke something or someone, to brush items out of your path, or if needed a cane can be used as a weapon.

Here's an idea. Use a walking stick for 24 hours. Take it with you when shopping, go to the mall, or any appointments you have for the day. Note people's reactions both positive and negative – then write about them. Do the same route another day sans cane. Do you notice any difference in the way you are treated?

I can't say I have enjoyed this forced change of viewpoint, yet it has been an interesting experiment. When you aren't in control of your world, life takes on a different face. Mundane becomes a challenge. Routine becomes struggle. Something to consider when creating characters or in fictional world building. I don't think I will ever look at anyone who walks with a cane or uses a wheelchair in the same way. My respect for their determination has gone up considerably.

In fact, I am thinking of creating a character that solves murders from a wheelchair. Whoops I think that's been done with Ironsides. Perhaps then a character temporarily confined to a chair and solves cases by keen observation. What a minute! I think Agatha Christie did that once with Miss Marple or maybe it was Hercule Poirot.

The message here is change your point of view by changing your view point. Whether you choose third person and narrate, first person and limit yourself, or omniscient and know everything, viewing the characters sideways, cockeyed, or upside-down changes things. Heck! If I can't be original, perhaps I'll invent a crotchety old lady who fends off a bear armed only with a designer walking stick and a bottle of Chanel No. 5. I know it has a few problems, I am confident that I can make it work.

Good advice. If I listened earlier, I wouldn't be here. But that's just the trouble with me. I give myself very good advice, but I very seldom follow it. Alice in Wonderland, 1951, Lewis Carroll.

Chapter 22

Everybody Has a Story

On Miller's third birthday, our grandson asked, "Mimi, what number are you?" I showed him ten fingers multiple times. Miller's eyes widened; I am sure he thought that I was joking. My three score plus years was too much to comprehend. Someone said, *Wisdom is taking the divine truth and applying it to everyday life.* Certainly, one of those divine truths is that everyone – even little Miller – has a story. But. the second part is even more exciting.

As a writer, I get to tell those stories. I wrote about Garnet and Frieda Carter, a couple who created a place of magic and wonder called Rock City. I was privileged to share my experiences with beginning writers, and I romped with kangaroos in the outback, chronicled our family's ongoing struggle with a special needs' grandson, and began baby steps toward blogging.

One of my columns was picked up by a New

York newspaper. Another time I got to be a cover girl for the Chattanooga Times. I won an award for a travel tip, toured Fernbank Science Center, Georgia's Wine Country, and Agatha's Mystery Dinner Theatre for research on articles. I attended the Atlanta Louvre exhibition, updated my knowledge of King Tut, and slept in the passenger car of the authentic Chattanooga Choo Choo on its hundredth birthday. And that's just me!

A vet shared his pilgrimage to Viet Nam thirty-seven years after the war. He and some fellow soldiers began an orphanage and have funded it all these years. His dream was twofold (1) locate the grave of a relative and (2) find as many of those orphans who are now adults as possible. My friend is seeking a much overdue reunion. He is journaling all of this and I have pledged to help with publishing his adventure.

Another writing buddy began writing her way through a tragedy and wound up a novelist of 1st rank. Still another is keeping a log and plans to publish her victory over dark areas in her life.

Our foster son has a story – one of abandonment, reinstatement, with numerous twists along the way. Some stories have a happy ending; others don't. Either way there are tears. There are always tears.

A brilliant colleague of my husband's told of his learning disability. He had compensated so well that no one ever guessed. Another professional revealed his dyslexia. A wonderful Christian woman secretly taught another how to read. There wasn't a dry eye in the house as she read the Christmas story aloud for the first time.

A family in our community lost loved ones in the tragedy of 911. Another donates dental equipment to clinics in Africa; our ophthalmologists volunteers on Tuesday evenings to a free clinic and spends summers on mission trips. And on it goes. Everyone has a story. Our job is to listen. Not just hear but **listen.** If we can manage that, maybe we will be entrusted with that person's story and give it to the world.

Remember Miller. I told you even at his young age, **he** had a story. When he was less than a year old, the doctors told my daughter they were convinced he had cystic fibrosis. He was very thin and not gaining weight at a normal rate even though his appetite was good. After a battery of tests, his pediatrician decided to change his formula one more time. Miller's mom is a nurse. She knew what cystic fibrosis would mean both to Miller and to the family. The entire family, church, and community prayed for Miller. We prayed like we hadn't prayed before. My daughter fed Miller around the clock, so that he would get all the nutrients on a regular cycle. That's the first time in my life I have prayed for someone to gain weight!

But at the end of the month, the doctor said Miller had not only gained three pounds, but his other symptoms of cystic fibrosis were gone! He is now a rambunctious athlete who wins medals in archery.

Remember my axiom: **Everybody's got a story.** Look at your family, your family history, friends, acquaintances, doctors, community leaders, the famous and the infamous. Perhaps you will be privileged to tell their story- or better still one of your own.

Chapter 23

Use What You've Got

When people learn you are a writer, some ephemeral urge causes them to "share" things with you. When I first launched my freelance career, I found it annoying that total strangers thrust their accounts of what cute thing their grandchild said, where they went on their summer vacation, or share a foolproof method of how to pick a ripe melon. As a published author, I felt I was "above" such mundane and everyday chit-chat. However, like so many of my other assumptions, I was wrong.

People want to read about other people. If that weren't so, *People, US, Style, Star, The National Enquirer*, and a host of other publications would be out of business tomorrow. And even if we don't read it, we listen to it and watch it. Broadcasters thrive on this kind of stuff. Births? Adoptions? Marriages? Break ups? You name it. People are news.

True the lady in Wal-Mart who related that her granddaughter insists on inheriting the family's gun collection is not celebrity stuff. It is interesting none the less. And writers know that stories concerning children sell.

If you are in a mind warp for ideas, think about links to other lands. In my own family I have ties to South Africa, Kenya, Zambia, Haiti, Afghanistan, and Norway. I recall stories passed down about my grandfather in World War I and my father in World War II. Stories about soldiers, hardship, and war romance situations sell.

With seven grandsons, someone is always entertaining, getting an award, getting injured, celebrating something, or going through drama. Drama sells. We love to hear about wrestling with a loose tooth, battling imaginary monsters, or celebrating an accomplishment. Dramas big and small are worth writing about.

Another way to use what you've got is to recall illnesses and recovery, prayers answered, losses or gains, celebrations, times of grief, or confidences betrayed. Childhood alone could fill volumes and may require sifting through what you want to reveal and what you don't. There are remembrances of those I hold dear, treasures lost, joy shared, memories of best friends, and the list goes on.

Any subject that brings tears while you write it will touch the heart of the reader. And that's also true with humor though humor is trickier to write. As Darrell Huckaby, syndicated columnist for the Atlanta Journal/Constitution columnist, says, "don't tell a funny story, tell a story funny."

When I fractured my foot, I wrote "Booty Call." When I got an ear plug stuck on vacation I wrote "Unplugged in Hawaii." When I washed my husband's hearing aid, I wrote "Miracle Err." You get the idea.

Then there are the heroes in your own community. My dentist donates dental chairs and equipment to free clinics in Africa. My ophthalmologist donates eye exams at Mercy Clinic and goes on medical mission trips. Our neighbor was gunned down by a crazed professor. A family in our town lost their children and grandchildren in the horrendous attacks on 911.

Sometimes stories come from our family's senior citizens. Those who have lived through difficult situations – war, depression, concentration camps – for instance. There are those who are caretakers, confidants, and those too shy to champion a cause. Those are the stories we look for and are anxious to tell.

I have a friend who served in Viet Nam. He and his soldier buddies began an orphanage to aid in the despair they saw in the lives of the children who were left to fend for themselves. This year he returned to the area for a reunion with the children who are now middle aged. But instead of coming home, he pulled up stakes and decided to spend the rest of his life where his heart was.

And if all else fails, there's the sixth-degree theory that we are one step away from each person that we know and two steps away from each person who is known by one of the people they know. The bottom line is that we are at most six steps away from any other person on Earth. Fascinating. I wonder how many degrees I am from Cleopatra or Catherine Zeta Jones? Story fodder for sure.

Chapter 24

The Self-Publishing Milieu

It is a great time to be a writer. Options are limited only by our imagination. We can blog, write columns, telecommute to work, enter contests online, and even get paid via PayPal. It is certainly no wonder then the self-publishing business is taking off.

Before you decide which route, suits your writing needs, wise authors such as yourselves must look at some statistics that I found -- where else but on the Internet?

When I first began my writing career, the term vanity press was used for writers who paid for getting their stuff published. A lesser extreme was the *subsidy press*, where the writer shared the cost of production with the publisher.

According to Publishers Weekly columnist Paul Nathan, "*Gone are the days when self-publishing was virtually synonymous with self-defeating."* And to prove it, Publishers Weekly now reviews books that are self-published. Something they wouldn't have done a few years ago.

John Kremer, Author of *Self-Publishing Hall of Fame,* reminds us that we could stock a "superb college library or an incredible bookstore just from the books written by some of the authors who have chosen to self-publish their books at some point in their lives."

Imagine my surprise to find poets – e. e. cummings, Percy B. Shelley, and Elizabeth Barrette Browning among the listings in the Self-Publishing Hall of Fame. They were alongside Mark Twain, Zane Grey, L. Frank Baum, and Pat Conroy. Savvy writers will recognize William Strunk and E. B. White who wrote The Elements of Style.

Margaret Atwood, William Blake, Lord Byron, Stephen Crane, Alexander Dumas, T. S. Eliot, Benjamin Franklin, Ernest Hemingway, Nathaniel Hawthorne, Stephen King, Rudyard Kipling, are only a few of the headliners.

I can't help but think how our education would have been diminished if these illustrious scribes had not published their works for posterity. Mr. Kremer has taken the time to research and catalog over 400 creative people who "at some point in their careers chose self-publishing as a legitimate option."

Like many other things in our life, it comes down to a personal choice. You alone can make that decision for your manuscript, book, play, anthology, memoir or poem collection. But it is important to keep our options open and weigh counsel of those we respect.

Of all Mr. Kremer's stories, the one I like best is that of Willa Cather. Willa was inspired by reading her cousin's wartime letters written to his mother. First Officer Cather from Nebraska was killed in World War I. Afterwards Willa wrote *One of Ours* which she self- published in 1922 based on those letters. *One of Ours* was awarded the <u>Pulitzer Prize</u> in 1923. The original letters are in the George Cather Ray Collection at the <u>University of Nebraska-Lincoln Libraries</u>.

We never know where the publishing road may lead. A small publisher gave John Grisham a shot, but he had to sell the copies of his first novel from the trunk of his car. William P. Young astounded everyone with his self-published novel, *The Shack*. It became a best seller and a major motion picture.

I've often wondered what would have happened if Mark Twain had owned a laptop or better still what if Stephen Crane had possessed a digital camera. Our entire cultural heritage would be different.

Chapter 25

Stay in Love

I love writing. I love the swirl and swing of words as they tangle with human emotions. James Michener

Being married for 50 years to the same man entails a daily decision to remain in love. I could arise, get dressed, and drive all the way to Cape Horn or I could arise, get dressed, and fix breakfast. It's my decision.

Being a writer is the same. You must stay in love with the sound of words, the smell of toner cartridges, and the click of nails on the keyboard. Sometimes the piece you are working on is like life: it doesn't turn out quite as we expected. But when that happens, take the long view. Perhaps the final story is better than the one we originally planned.

If you win an award for a manuscript, then you deserve congratulations for hard work, planning, and perseverance. On the other hand, if your story didn't make the cut, remember that winners are based on one person's opinion, on one piece, at one time, and not a universal pronouncement on your talent.

Writing is a solitary career. And as such we take ourselves and our accomplishments very seriously. Our strong points are also our weak ones. Talent is needed but the real key to getting published and making writing more than a hobby is perseverance.

Perseverance is the key to long life, a lasting marriage, and a writing career without an expiration date. Not a person I know hasn't wanted to give up on something whether it is a wayward child, a nowhere career, a bad marriage, or a dream that doesn't seem like it would ever come true. If your heart is telling you to hang tough when it isn't logical, recommended, or even smart, you may be onto something.

I have a friend who is an actress. Cheri has performed on stage, screen, and television. When I interviewed her, I asked for advice to would-be actors. "If you can be anything else, don't be an actor," she advised.

Good advice for writers as well. Writing is solitary – sometimes lonely. You must be able to stay true to your vocation and go the distance. In short: you must stay in love with the craft.

Chapter 26

Take a Shower

Writer's block is a scourge for the writing community. Many writer friends declare that writers' block melts while strolling in the park. On the other hand, a graphospasm for words may dissolves while mowing the lawn or cruising the interstate.

One pal of mine entertains her muse in a "quiet" room complete with incense and earth sounds. A mentor once shared with me that her ideas regularly gurgle forth at 5:00 a.m. and on rare occasions spew into overdrive after midnight.

Not me. My ideas are most potent when taken with water. Lots of water. Preferably mixed with a potion from Bath and Body. You see I get my most clever ideas while I am in the shower.

Funny scenarios parade before me when I lather

up in Juniper Breeze. Juvenile stories worthy of a Newberry Medal impress themselves into my brain while soaking in Peach Nectar. Plumeria conjures up an eruption at Kilauea as palm trees and hula dancers sway in the sunset.

Chapter by chapter an entire novel comes alive complete with plot, subplots, brilliant synopsis, and twist endings. All while I wash away the grime of my day. Clever first lines and stunning closures present themselves for approval in a myriad of subjects while Toasted Almond reminds me of a childhood adventure at my grandparents' farm when my cousin and I released a prize bull. Warm trickles of foam down my back renew the pleasures of an Amsterdam vacation complete with trespassing charges. Shampooing my hair is not unlike lathering a menagerie of pets willed to us by some spiteful fairy of mentally challenged animals.

Writing under the influence of my shower muse is joyously inspirational. But there are definite drawbacks -- such as note taking. I experimented with placing pads of paper on the bathroom counter only to emerge from the bath amid disintegrating blobs of paper with faded ink puddles.

One stroke of brilliance was to take a small recorder into the bath. I switched it on to record my dynamic thoughts only to have them drowned out by sounds of water spraying on the ceramic tile. The only workable solution I have found is to rehearse the thoughts conceived during my beauty regime by constantly repeating them until I can rinse, towel off, and capture them onto my laptop.

Alas, the process loses something in the

translation. Too often, I scratch my head and wonder what I was so excited about. Writing with a shower muse is messy, shrivels the skin, and is inconvenient. Yet he persists in visiting my bath despite my attempts to lure him into the study.

One thing I have realized after one of our rendezvous, my writing is squeaky clean.

Chapter 27

My Trip Down the Rabbit Hole

I could tell you my adventures beginning from this morning," said Alice a little timidly: "but it's no use going back to yesterday, because I was a different person then. <u>Alice's Adventures in Wonderland</u> by Lewis Carroll

On July 28th, 2010 I embarked upon a most bizarre adventure. My husband, Tim, registered into St. Mary's Hospital for a simple procedure. By 10:30 a.m., Dr. Bhatt, the pulmonologist, reported all was going well with his heart catheterization. He explained that Tim would be in recovery for an hour, but that's where he was wrong.

A vein in Tim's heart tore as Dr. Tongia, the cardiologist, inserted a stent. Just like that, we were in for the ride of a lifetime. An ambulance transported Tim to Athens Regional for emergency open heart surgery.

After four hours of surgery, my husband entered the Cardiovascular Intensive Care Unit. Dr. Morris, the cardiovascular surgeon, held out little hope of him ever leaving the unit and certainly not without brain damage. Miraculously, on the eighth day Tim sat up in bed and asked for the television remote.

Step down followed with medical staff and well-meaning volunteers who walked me through what my future would hold for the next six to twelve months. Ten days of physical rehabilitation followed making Tim's total stay a hefty twenty-three days. St. Mary's Home Health Care peopled with Occupational and Physical Therapists have been caring for Tim twice a week ever since.

Survivors tell me that this is only the beginning. Cardiac Rehab follows immediately after this and only after graduation may we return to our somewhat "normal lifestyle." Hooked up to 19 different tubes, machines, and medicines, my emotions stretched taut and ran from despair to hope to ecstasy to anger and remorse. Some emotions are still too raw to reveal. My high respect for nursing has escalated. Dedicated, wonderful people cared for all of us – in and out of the hospital room.

A wake-up call like ours sets priorities. First. Love Rules. Love for God, family, and friends has always been a priority but now is priority one. Only by being surrounded with love could I have withstood the pressures of praying for the best while fearing the worst.

Secondly, at my darkest moment faith took control. I chose to believe God's ministering spirits were protecting Tim even when I couldn't be there. Psalm 91 became my mantra and source of great comfort.

Third, my patience has increased in some areas and decreased in others. I have all the time in the world for a hurting soul but no time for a grumbling one.

I posted on **Facebook**: "I feel like Alice when she fell through the Rabbit Hole except it took 23 days to complete my journey."

My writer friend, Charlotte, in her wisdom, replied "Yes, but you came through it and became the White Queen."

White Queen or not. I know that my journey was for a reason. Perhaps it was for others who find themselves on the same journey. I hope that I never forget what the trip down the rabbit hole taught me.

If you, fellow writers, find yourself going into the abyss, give me a call. I am personal friends with the Mad Hatter. Visit and we'll all have tea.

Sheila S. Hudson
161 Woodstone Drive

Athens GA 30605
706-296-7056

sheilahudson.writer@gmail.com

www.sheilahudson.website.com

Activities:

Southeastern Writers' Association, 1993-Present; SWA Board Member
Infinite Writer – Columnist 2008

Purple Pros – Columnist 1997 – 2005
Grand Magazine – Columnist 2010
University of Georgia: Learning in Retirement –
Instructor

Books:

Classic City Murders (2) Thomas Max Publishers

Ministry Can Be Murder series (2) Winged Publications

Silent Partner series (3) Winged Publications

The Thursday Club series (7) Winged Publications

13 Decisions That Will Change Your Life, Dancing with Bear Publishing

13 Decisions That Will Transform Your Marriage, Dancing with Bear Publishing

Current Publications:

Writing Opens Doors, Boom Magazine, 2018.

Pray Expectantly, Christian Standard, 2011.

Waiting for a Miracle, Christian Standard, 2011.

A Tale of Tea Cakes, Grit Magazine, 2010.

Grandma's Glasses, Patchwork Path, Treasure Box, 2010.

Grandfather's Ring, Patchwork Path, Treasure Box, 2010.

Gift of Normandy Beach, Patchwork Path, Christmas Stocking, 2010.

Home Grown Talent, Athens Magazine, January 2010.

Did God Make Michael Wrong? Athens Parent, March 2009.

Forgiveness: Not an Option, Lookout Magazine, Nov. 2, 2008.

Transform, Athena Magazine, March 2008.

PLEASE CONTACT ME ABOUT WRITING AND SPEAKING OPPORTUNITIES. ALL BOOKS ARE AVAILABLE ON AMAZON.COM

Made in the USA
Columbia, SC
02 May 2019